TIME

MANAGEMENT

TIME MANAGEMENT

CONQUERING THE CLOCK

Dr. Barrie Hopson
and Mike Scally

Pfeiffer
& COMPANY

Amsterdam • Johannesburg • London
San Diego • Sydney • Toronto

Published in association with

Publisher: Pfeiffer/Mercury Books

Published in the UK by Mercury Books. This edition published by:
Pfeiffer & Company
8517 Production Avenue
San Diego, CA 92121-2280 USA

This publication is designed to provide accurate and authori-
tative information in regard to the subject matter covered. It
is sold with the understanding that the publisher is not
engaged in rendering legal, accounting, or other professional
service. If legal advice or other expert assistance is required,
the services of a competent professional person should be
sought. *From a Declaration of Principles jointly adopted by a
Committee of the American Bar Association and a Committee of
Publishers.*

Editor: Arlette C. Ballew
Page Compositor: Nicola Ruskin
Cover: John Odam Design Associates

Library of Congress Cataloging-in-Publication Data
Hopson, Barrie.
 Time management: conquering the clock/Barrie Hopson,
Mike Scally.
  p. cm.
  ISBN 0-89384-213-3
  1. Time management—United States—Handbooks, manuals,
etc.
 I. Scally, Mike. II. Title.
 HN90.T5H67   1993
 640'.43–dc20   92-50997

Printed in the United States of America.
Printing 1 2 3 4 5 6 7 8 9 10

Contents

Preface

Welcome to our series of open learning workbooks. In this brief preface, we invite you to consider some of our beliefs.

- **We do not need teachers to learn.** Not all of what we know in life was learned through formal education. We can, and do, learn in a wide range of ways, and we learn best when we know our own needs.

- **The best way to help people is to encourage them to help themselves.** Self-help and self-management avoid the dependency that blocks development and burdens ourselves and others.

- **Awareness, knowledge, and skills give us more options in life.** Lack of any of these is a disadvantage; possession of them allows us to live fuller lives, shaping events rather than simply reacting to them.

- **The more able and accomplished we become, the more we fill society's reservoir of talent and contribute to the common good.**

- **It has been said that the future is not what it used to be!** In this age, the goalposts keep being moved, so increasingly our security needs to come from having information and skills.

The term "lifeskill" came from work based on these beliefs, which we began at Leeds University in the 1970s. Our philosophy has been widely applied in education, in industry and commerce, and in the community, inviting people to take charge of their lives and make them satisfying and rewarding.

Lifeskills have, so far, been available through training courses and teaching programs. Now they are available in a self-help format that is consistent with the Lifeskills approach, because you are in charge of your own learning. Learn at your own pace, in your own time, and apply your learning to your situation. We wish you both enjoyment and success!

Barrie Hopson
Mike Scally

Introduction

This book is for people who care about personal development. It involves reading and doing, so we have written it as an open learning workbook.

Open learning describes a study program that is designed so that it adapts to the needs of individual learners. Some open learning programs involve attendance at a study center of some kind, or contact with a tutor or mentor, but even then attendance times are flexible and suit the individual. This workbook is for you to use at home or at work. Most of the activities are for you to complete alone. Sometimes we may suggest that you talk with a friend or colleague—self-development is easier if there is another person with whom to talk over ideas. But this isn't essential by any means.

With this workbook you can

- Organize your study to suit your own needs.
- Study the material alone or with other people.
- Work through the book at your own pace.
- Start and finish when and where you want to, although we have indicated suggested stopping points with a ☕ symbol.

The sections marked "Personal Project" involve you in more than working through the text, they require you to take additional time—sometimes an evening, sometimes a week. For this reason, we do not suggest specifically how long it will take you to complete this workbook, but the written part of the book will probably take you about six hours to complete.

Objectives

During this self-help program, you will

- Become aware of how you presently use your time.
- Prioritize the ways in which you use your time.
- Rank your priorities in order of importance.
- Explore the concepts of sold time, maintenance time, and discretionary time.
- Develop your skills in managing time.

What Is Time Management?

"I'd really like to go swimming on Thursday, but I'm afraid I simply haven't got the time."

"Yes, I'd love to start that new project, but I've got a thousand and one things to finish first."

"I'm sorry to break our date, but I really must complete that report for tomorrow morning."

"Perhaps we could meet two weeks from Wednesday; that's the first free day I have."

Do the above statements sound familiar? If you find yourself talking like this too often, you really need to make some changes and conquer the clock!

Time management involves setting clear priorities for yourself and making sure that you achieve them. Time is a limited resource, so you have to make choices. When the time is gone, it's gone! Learn how to conquer the clock now.

We hope that by the end of this workbook, you will no longer think, "I would like to do that but I haven't got the time." You will either arrange to do it or think, "I could do that, but I like what I'm doing a lot better!"

Three key words can help you to achieve better management of your time.

- **Knowledge:** You need to know clearly what you need or want to do.
- **Choice:** You need to make a choice among these.
- **Time:** You need to schedule time to act on your choice.

The important skill that this program emphasizes is your ability to establish priorities and to apportion time to achieve them. It offers you the opportunity to explore techniques for planning your time more effectively so that you can accomplish all your important priorities, some of your less important priorities, and even a few of the relatively unimportant ones.

We realize that life is full of unexpected surprises, so another important element in this program is flexibility. Indeed, this workbook itself is flexible: You choose when and how you use it. By the time you have reached the end of the book, we hope that you will be able to choose and use your time more efficiently.

Managing Time Does Not Mean Always Being Busy

We are not suggesting that every minute of your time must be packed with activity, but that it is possible to get what you want out of as much time as you have. That includes planning for relaxation.

What Would You Like to Get From This Workbook?

Before you move on to the first chapter, take about five minutes to think about what you would like to achieve by completing this workbook and what you hope to get out of it. Note three things you find frustrating about the way you

Time Management Is About Priorities

↓

Priorities Result From Setting Objectives

↓

Setting Objectives Is About Planning

↓

Planning Is About Control

↓

Being in Control Is Being Self-Empowered

↓

Self-Empowered People Manage Their Time

currently spend your time (e.g., Are you often late? Do you find it difficult to get certain things done? Do you feel that all your time belongs to other people?).

1. _____

2. _____

3. _____

Now let your imagination loose for a few minutes to think about the possibilities that you could open up for yourself. What are your personal objectives in doing this workbook?

Write your objectives below.

_____

_____

_____

_____

_____

One important thing that I would really like to achieve that
I don't have time for currently is _____

_____

Two things that I would like to change about the way I spend
my time are

1. _____

_____

2. _____

_____

Now that you have begun to identify your personal goals, we
suggest that you keep returning to what you have written as
you go through this workbook. Reviewing your objectives
regularly will help you to monitor your progress. It will also
help you to choose the time-management techniques that are
most helpful to you. Don't hesitate to change or add to your
objectives as you work through the chapters; your ideas will
change with your progress!

1

Life
Investment
Record

The objective of this chapter is to
help you to become aware of how
you actually spend your time.

The key to time management is knowing how to spend your time. You have 24 hours available each day. Regard them as a stock of investment funds; where you invest them determines what you get in return from the day.

First, it is important to find out how you really spend your time. You can do this by completing the following Life Investment Record, which lists your activities for every hour in the week. This will provide you with basic information that will help you to make choices about time later on in this workbook.

Personal Project:
Life Investment Record and Activity Charts

The following Life Investment Record splits the days of the week into two-hour periods. We suggest that you fill in the record over the next seven consecutive days. You will need to complete a full week (seven 24-hour periods) of Life Investment Records before you can proceed with the other chapters in this program.

We have found that recording your time in two-hour blocks is effective, but you can split the chart into whatever time periods suit you, although these should not be too large. Every night, enter into the record what you did during the day. It is important to make your entries regularly each day, because it is very easy to forget what you have done.

Life Investment Record

	Mon	Tue	Wed	Thu	Fri	Sat	Sun
AM 12-2							
2-4							
4-6							
6-8							
8-10							
10-12							
PM 12-2							
2-4							
4-6							
6-8							
8-10							
10-12							

You may find it helpful to keep a log, jotting down things as you do them during the day. You will still need to transfer your entries into the Life Investment Record at the end of the week to provide an overview of how you spent your time. An overview is very important, as it will allow you to look back and identify time-use patterns. When you have completed your Life Investment Record for a week, you will be able to analyze how your time was spent.

In the Time Activity Chart that follows, list the activities described in your Life Investment Record (for example, sleeping, eating, caring for children, watching television, shopping, cooking, domestic tasks, driving, or being at work). If you have a job, you may find it useful to break down how you spend your time at work. Use subheadings for your different work activities (for example, talking on the telephone, attending meetings, photocopying, or traveling).

Next, figure out how many hours you spent on each activity. Enter this figure in the space provided, to the right of the activity.

Time Activity Chart

Activity	Number of Hours Spent
Eating	
Child Care	
Sleeping	
Traveling	
Shopping	
Domestic Chores	
Cooking	
Working	

Spend a few minutes looking over your chart. Then rank your activities using the Rank Order Activity Chart. Put the activity with the greatest number of hours next to the 1, put the activity with the next highest number of hours next to the 2, and so on.

Rank Order Activity Chart

Activity	Number of Hours Spent
1.	
2.	
3.	
4.	
5.	
6.	
7.	
8.	
9.	
10.	
11.	
12.	
13.	
14.	
15.	
16.	
17.	
18.	
19.	
20.	

Look over your chart and think about the following questions:

What surprises you about the way you have spent your week?

_____

_____

_____

Was there anything unusual about this particular week?

_____

_____

_____

What return are you getting on your investment, i.e., how satisfied are you?

_____

_____

_____

What changes would you like to make?

_____

_____

_____

Can you see ways to save time so that you could invest it in something else? If so, what are they?

_____

_____

_____

Are there any gaps where you cannot recall what you were doing?

_____

_____

_____

Summary

You now have an analysis of how you actually spent a week of your life. It may have produced some surprises for you! For example, the amount of time spent watching television or walking the dog might be much greater than you thought. Maybe you spent less time on the briefcase full of "homework" than you had thought. Even if your Life Investment Record turned out as you expected, there will be opportunities for you to spend more time on some activities and less time on others.

In the next chapter, you will look at your Life Investment Record in more detail, so that you can start identifying areas where you might save time or put it to better use.

You will never have that week again. Are you happy about the ways in which you spent your time?

2

Time Check

The objectives of this chapter
are to increase your awareness
of how you spend your time and
to develop your skills and
techniques in managing time.

Our lives are constantly changing. We develop as individuals, our interests diversify, and the circumstances around us alter. As a result, we need to regularly review our use of time, to ensure that what we do corresponds with what we want to do.

Time Charts

Use the following questionnaire to review your use of time last week. Make an honest assessment, as the point of the activity is to identify what you did well and what you can improve.

It might be useful to ask a co-worker or family member to assess your time management skills. Just remember that you solicited their input and try not to react negatively to what you perceive as criticisms. Use the box below to record an observer's feedback.

My Use of Time Last Week

Overall impressions of how I have spent the week.

How much time have I given to what I enjoy?

How much time have I spent on what I don't enjoy?

Have I wasted time? How much? How?

How much time was given to what I think is important?

Did I constructively use the time I spent waiting or traveling?

How much time did I allocate to my priorities?

Did I know each day what I wanted to achieve?

(continued)

Did anything that I wanted to do get postponed?

Have I used any time particularly successfully this week? Can I build on this next week?

Have I spent time on routines or habits that I would like to break?

Have I given myself a reward for time well spent?

Have I set some deadlines for myself and met them?

Have I wasted other people's time? If so, how?

Have I found time to relax?

Have I asked frequently, "What is the best use of my time right now?"

What do your answers tell you about how you used your time last week?

_____

_____

_____

Is there anything you might want to change next week?

_____

_____

_____

Personal Project: Weekly Time Checks

Try doing a time-check review every week. We have included a sample Daily Time Chart so that you can see the kind of things to include. This chart is especially helpful if you work, but you also should include time spent outside working hours.

It is a good idea to keep your Daily Time Charts together so that you can review your progress and identify recurring features. Later on, we will look at the techniques of using a time management personal planner.

Summary

In this chapter, you began to think about how you really use your time. Chapter 3 will let you go into more detail and find out how to plan to use time for the things you enjoy.

Daily Time Chart

Time	Activity
8:50	Cup of tea. Searched for missing letter. Did some filing, too.
9:25	Couple of people wanting to talk.
9:35	Begin meeting with Mike on posters to accompany a book. It's hard to decide what we want.
10:05	Typesetter arrives; we all three look at boards.
10:35	Publishing team meeting, followed by "debriefing" session with M.D.
11:50	Cup of coffee, chat with Ann Marie. Karen is ill, so sent her home!
12:30	Back to poster meeting and reading typeset boards.
1:00	Continue poster concept meeting at lunch.
1:45	Pick up boards again.
2:15	Barrie telephoned, leaving messages, etc.
2:35	Glanced through two magazines (<u>HRD Quarterly</u>, <u>Training Tomorrow</u>).
2:50	Photocopy our drafts and ideas for poster. Start layout.
3:50	Designs for new catalogue cover arrive. Peter, Michael, and I look at them.
4:05	Mike briefs me on publication schedule of NOW books.
4:30	Make two phone calls. Get together to celebrate two birthdays.
5:00	Return to layout for 20 minutes. Write out tasks for tomorrow.
5:45	Leave office.

3

Time and Satisfaction

The objectives of this chapter
are to identify how you
presently spend your time and
prioritize the ways in which you
use your time.

I n this chapter we will look at the central problem in time management—how well we match what we want to do with what we actually do. The aim is to increase the time you spend on satisfying activities as a proportion of all time spent.

To do this, you need to know how you actually spend your time now and how you could spend your time in order to give yourself the greatest satisfaction and pleasure. Let's look at a technique for doing this.

Satisfying Activities

In the box that follows, make a list of the activities that satisfy you. Define satisfaction in your own terms, but use only those activities that you actually do now. This will vary greatly among individuals. So make your list one that shows what actually satisfies you, not what you think it "ought to be."

Satisfying Activities

A pie chart can show the activities that satisfy you and the *relative satisfaction* you get from each activity. Everyone's Satisfaction Pie is different. Look at the two different examples; your pie chart will probably contain many activities that are different from these examples.

Sample Satisfaction Pies

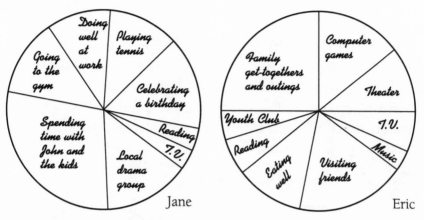

Jane   Eric

Now enter your satisfying activities on the blank pie chart that follows, with each activity as a slice of the pie. The more *satisfying* the activity, the larger its slice of the pie. The complete pie is a synopsis of your satisfying life activities.

Your Satisfaction Pie

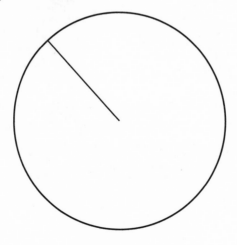

One point the pie chart makes clear is that you can increase the time you devote to one satisfying activity only at the expense of time devoted to another activity. This means that you have to make *choices*.

Spend a minute or two looking at your Satisfaction Pie. Then go on to the next stage, which looks at the amount of *time you actually spend* on each of your satisfying activities.

Time Spent on Satisfying Activities

We have shown you Jane's and Eric's Satisfaction Pies; following are their Actual-Time Pies. As you can see, there are discrepancies. For example, like many of us, they both watch more television than the satisfaction they get from that activity warrants!

Sample Actual-Time Pies

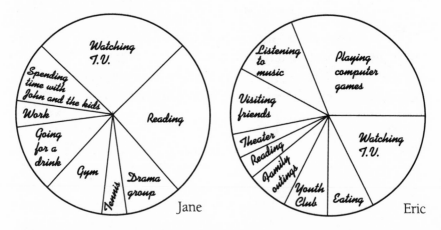

On the Actual-Time Pie that follows, enter the amount of time you now spend on your satisfying activities. This time, the size of the slice indicates the actual amount of time spent in proportion to other activities.

Your Actual-Time Pie

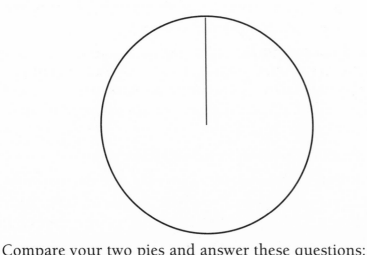

Compare your two pies and answer these questions:

Does anything surprise you about either of your pies?

_____

_____

_____

Are there any differences between your Satisfaction Pie and your Actual-Time Pie? What are they?

_____

_____

_____

What does this say about your current lifestyle?

_____

_____

_____

Compare the Satisfaction and Actual-Time Pies in our examples. Many of the things that Jane and Eric really enjoy and find satisfying are squeezed out by other activities.

Look back at your Life Investment Record in Chapter 1 and compare it with your two pies. Then spend about five minutes on the following two questions.

Are there any other satisfying activities in your Life Investment Record that you have forgotten to include in your Satisfaction Pie? Write down some thoughts about this below.

Your Actual-Time Pie shows the amount of time you *think* you spend on satisfying activities. Your Life Investment Record shows the amount of time you actually *spent* on those activities over one week. Is there any mismatch between the time you *think* you spend and the time you *actually* spend on satisfying activities? Write your thoughts below.

Your Ideal Satisfaction Pie

Your Ideal Actual-Time Pie

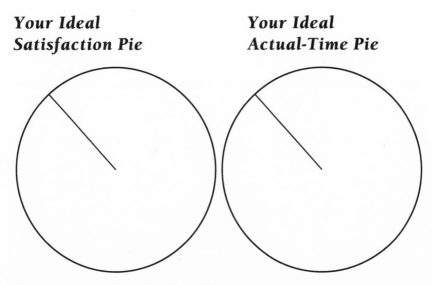

Summary: Pies in the Skies!

We have been asking you to focus on activities that you do now that you find satisfying. In the final part of this chapter, we invite you to use your imagination! In an ideal world, how would you spend your time? Above you will find a final set of pies. Using the same headings as in your original set of pies, fill in the Satisfaction Pie as you would like it to look and the Actual-Time Pie as you would like it to look.

By comparing your actual and your ideal sets of pies, you now know where you are and where you would like to be. You have the basic information for making time management decisions that will enable you to manage your time to your greater satisfaction. Today is the first day of the rest of your life, so make the most of it!

4

Identifying Priorities

The objective of this chapter is
to help you to identify priorities
in the ways in which you use
your time.

You have only 24 hours in a day. Time is limited, but the possible demands on it are infinite. If you are not simply to react to demands, you must choose how to allocate your time—to identify priorities. In the last chapter, you analyzed how you spent your time last week. Now you will consider how you plan to spend your time next week.

Creating a Priorities Chart

In the boxes that follow, write all the ideas that occur to you in response to the headings. Spend about three minutes on each topic. Don't try to put your answers in any order, simply note your ideas freely as they occur to you.

What I Have to Do Next Week

What I Want to Do Next Week

Take each list in turn and pick out the most important items that you have to do or want to do next week.

When you have done this, look over the items that you have selected. Ask yourself which of these items you are going to give the most priority to. Think through all the factors, the implications, and the pros and cons of each item and then decide which will be your number-one choice. Write this choice next to the 1 in the box that follows and then repeat the process for 2, 3, 4, and so on.

Priorities for This Week
1.
2.
3.
4.
5.
6.
7.
8.
9.
10.

Now that you have created your list of priorities, you may find it helpful to copy it and keep it where you will see it frequently during the next week.

Review the list two or three times during the week and strike through items when you have done them. You will find that some items are no longer priorities—they have resolved themselves or changed. Your list will alter accordingly. What is left undone on the list at the end of the week can be included in the priorities you set for the following week.

At the end of next week, review your list of priorities and then answer the following questions. Use a friend or colleague as a consultant if you find it helpful.

How aware am I of my priorities?

_____

_____

How much am I choosing/initiating?

_____

_____

Am I proactive or reactive? (Do I make things happen or let things happen to me?)

_____

_____

Summary

We have looked at the principle of identifying priorities and have begun to explore techniques for doing this. In the next chapter, we will look at another useful technique for ranking priorities in order of importance.

5

Effective List Making

The objective of this chapter is
to look at techniques for
ranking priorities in order of
importance.

W e all have important things to do in our lives, but how do we remember how and when to do them? Trusting to memory is one way, but, unfortunately, it is not very reliable. It also increases anxiety. Relying on someone else to remind you means handing over responsibility for your life to someone else, which is not very self-empowered behavior! One satisfactory way of guaranteeing that you achieve your priorities is by making an effective list.

Some people believe that list making is tedious and one more way to waste time rather than save it. We suggest that you weigh up the advantages and disadvantages of list making for yourself. We've listed some advantages, but there's space for you to list some of your own. By filling in your own lists of advantages and disadvantages you can quickly see which side outweighs the other.

List Making as a Tool for Time Management	
Advantages	**Disadvantages**
Takes away anxiety about forgetting to do things.	
Having it on paper ensures that you don't forget.	
Helps you to figure out what is important.	
Provides an immediate progress report on what you have achieved.	

Your disadvantages might have included that lists take too long to compile, that they might not be comprehensive, and what happens if you lose your list. Despite these disadvantages, we still think that lists really can help you manage your time. So here are some tips on effective list making.

Where to Start

We suggest that you do this exercise at the end of the day, when you can start to plan ahead. Spend about five minutes considering what you'd like to achieve tomorrow. In the space that follows, make a list of all the things you *have* to do tomorrow and all the things you *want* to do tomorrow.

Things I *have* to do tomorrow

_____

_____

_____

Things I *want* to do tomorrow

_____

_____

_____

Now work out your priorities by coding the items on the list into three categories:

A. Things you must do or want to do tomorrow.
B. Things you should do or would like to do by the end of the day.
C. Things you would like to do by the end of the day, but it won't matter if you don't.

Write your list in the box, giving each item a letter code. Then number each item (A1, A2, etc.), according to how important it is.

As you go through your day, complete the A items first, then the Bs, and finally the Cs. Try out this system every day for a week, making a new list for each day.

Priorities List

You may find that this way of planning doesn't exactly suit you, so there are some tips after this that will give you some ideas for minor alterations. Feel free to adapt our Priorities List but don't forget that, however you do your list, unpleasant jobs still have to be done!

Personal Project

Bear in mind these tips during this trial week.

- Make your new list at the end of each day, while you're still thinking about tasks to do for tomorrow.
- Keep the list with you.
- Cross off items when they've been achieved. This acts as a reward.
- Ask yourself from time to time, "Am I spending too much time on the B and C items?"
- As soon as something new occurs, add it to the list and letter code it.
- Do you have the right balance between what you must do and what you want to do? It's important to take care of some of your own needs.
- Ask yourself periodically, "Am I doing what I want to do right now?"
- Don't put off unpleasant jobs; they won't get any easier!
- When you've completed an A item that you must do, reward yourself by achieving one of your "wants."
- Transfer to tomorrow's list any uncompleted items from today.
- If a C item remains on your list for more than three or four days, either upgrade it to A or B or cross it off and forget about it!
- Remember to build in "thinking time" where necessary.
- Things like going shopping or writing reports often take longer than you think, so build in extra time (approximately 20 percent) if you can.
- Use short C jobs to act as energizers, or do one at the beginning of the day to get off to a successful start.

Summary

At the end of your trial week, ask yourself these questions:
How does a list help me; how does it hinder me?

_____

_____

_____

Did I forget anything?

_____

_____

_____

Did I get more done? If so, why?

_____

_____

_____

What did I do differently during the week when I made lists?

_____

_____

_____

You almost certainly will want to adapt your list-making techniques to suit your personal needs. But if you persist, you will find list making and prioritizing to be a powerful tool in organizing your time.

6

Using a
Personal
Planner or
Organizer

The objective of this chapter is
to introduce you to a powerful
time management aid.

As your time management skills develop, you will become aware that you have produced a number of lists and charts. These are the basic tools with which to plan your time. As with any tools, it helps if you keep them all together—a good place to do this is in a personal planner or organizer.

Most people are familiar with personal planners or organizers. They provide a convenient place to keep your daily lists, plus extra space to keep records and charts, and are essential for planning. However, you may prefer to use something larger and more roomy, a binder file or box, for instance. These are great for storing lots of information, but they are not very effective for detailed planning.

Planners need not be expensive; you can buy a notebook and customize it yourself. On the other hand, professionally produced planners are attractive and provide preprinted pages and charts. An advantage of many commercially available planners is their looseleaf binder system, which allows you to add and reposition pages as you like.

A possible disadvantage of planners is their size. Some of them are quite bulky. If size is important to you, choose a small, easily portable pocket calendar for essential daily information and a larger notebook for longer-term plans, charts, and diagrams. You may find that you use a box file for home organizing and a personal planner for work. Maybe a small pocket calendar would suffice if you were to put other information on an office wall chart. The important thing is to find something that suits you.

In the box that follows, write down a list of items to keep in your personal planner.

What kinds of things did you write down? Was it just appointments or did you also list decisions that need to be made? An advantage of listing decisions is that you can use your time more constructively because you won't be worrying for days about decisions that you need to make in the future.

Personal Planner Pages

The next two pages show examples of two personal planner calendar pages. As you will see, the first is for a week and contains items relating to both home and work. The second is a daily one and covers mainly work. The Appendix includes blank versions of the two calendar pages that you may reproduce and use. It might make sense for you to keep more than one planner, especially if you have a busy workday and a busy social life. If you are very involved in something like a political party or social club, you may want to keep a planner specifically for that.

Gather together all the charts and lists that you have produced to plan your time. Sort them into those that go in the calendar section and those that go in the planner section.

Weekly Calendar: *November 7 to November 13*

	Monday	Tuesday	Wednesday	Thursday	Friday	Saturday	Sunday
Morning	Prepared papers for afternoon meetings	Working at home	Working at home	9-12 Prepared report for board of directors meeting	Off to a furniture shop in Warrington with George	Go into town with children for shoes	Washing and ironing
Afternoon	12-2 meeting 2-4 meeting	Working at home	Lunch with Gill	1-4 Attended insurance seminar	Lunch with George Travel back		Walk with children
Evening	Watched television	Made a meal for Christine; chat	Stripped and varnished kitchen chairs	Late-night shopping	Collapse and fall asleep in front of the television	Prepared some delicious food from new cookbook	Painted legs of kitchen chairs

Monday, October 15

6AM	
7AM	
8AM	
Prepare presentation	9AM
	10AM
	11AM
Phone calls	NOON
Lunch	1PM
Presentation	2PM
	3PM
Mike: Review meeting	4PM
Dictation	5PM
	6PM
	7PM
Tennis: Jerry	8PM
	9PM
	10PM
	11PM
	MIDNIGHT

Action

Talk To

Mike: Review
Liz: Notes for
presentation

Dennis: Ideas
for new program?

Telephone

JoAnn Wirth: Job Interview

Moira re lunch

Book tennis court

Write To

Minutes: SPR
Meeting (see plans)

Norman Smith
re bookings

Notes

Pay bills
Do expenses!

Order stationery
- pens
- pads
- 12 binders

Enter them into the appropriate sections. Below is an example of how you could do this.

Calendar	Planner
Priorities List for the Week	Life Investment Record
Monthly Calendar	Activity Percentages Charts
Weekly Calendar	Satisfaction Pies
Yearly Calendar	Actual-Time Pies
	Use of Time This Week Charts
	Motivational Quotations or Aphorisms

Use the space below to decide where you will store your lists and charts.

Summary

Your planner has everything you need to plan a more satisfying life. It is important to remember that it can only help you if you actually use it. Try to arrange a definite time each week for your planning activities.

7

Creating an Efficient Working Environment

*The objective of this chapter is
to show you how an organized
workspace, office, or study can
help you manage your time.*

Although we use the words "office" and "desk" in this section, the principles of creating a good working environment apply just as well to a home. Think about the difference between working in a clean, well-organized kitchen and a messy, chaotic one. Household tasks need as much organizing as office work!

Imagine that you have an important job to do tomorrow. What would make you feel good about starting it? Jot down a few thoughts about your ideal working environment.

Your Ideal Working Environment

We think that the following things are important:

- A clear work space or desk—this lets you concentrate fully on the task.
- The right tools for the job—before you begin make sure that you have the right equipment, books, stationery,

supplies, files, and data. Then you won't waste valuable time searching for things.

- Peace and quiet (if possible!) – don't start an important job when you know that company is coming, the children are on their way home from school, or the telephone will be particularly busy.

- A comfortable work space – you can't concentrate if you're thinking about your aching back or smarting eyes. Try to work in good light, sitting in a comfortable chair, at a work surface that is the right height.

- A favorite picture on the wall or fresh flowers on your desk – when you need to take a break, look at these and let your mind wander and relax.

Of course, you should try to be organized all the time, not just when you have an important job to do! Knowing exactly where things are can save hours.

The basis of a time-efficient approach to many jobs is a good filing system. This isn't as technical as it sounds; most people "file" their household goods, for example, cleaning materials in one cabinet, food in another. Filing can mean anything from putting all the bills in an old shoe box or storing holiday photographs in a scrapbook to the more complex filing systems found in offices.

Filing Systems

Think for a few minutes about the kinds of filing systems, if any, that you use. Write them in the space that follows.

One excellent way of keeping track of information is to divide it into different sections. If you are working, you could try the six categories that follow; if you don't work, you probably will find that two or three of these categories will be enough. Use files or boxes to keep each section separate.

| File | Work that has been finished, but that needs to be kept for reference |

| Do now | Letters, bills, etc., that need action today |

| Do soon | Jobs that must be done soon but are not yet urgent |

| Read | Papers, magazines, and reports |

| Pass on | Information that needs to go to another person with some comment or advice |

| Awaiting information | Jobs that need further information before anything can be done |

If the system works, you will find that many jobs progress through most or all of these files. For example, an article that you must read comes in. You spot something that a colleague would be interested in and put it in the "do soon" file. The next day you move it to the "do now" file and you write a note, attach a copy of the article, and put the original article and a copy of the letter into the "awaiting information" file. Your friend writes back thanking you, so the letter and article now can be filed.

In and Out Trays

Trays can be very useful for keeping your papers all in one place. Make sure that any incoming letters, messages, or memos are put right into the in tray. Look at the in tray regularly and, if necessary, transfer items to your filing system. When mail is due to be sent or given directly to another person, put these items in the out tray.

Notice Boards

Notice boards are a great way of reminding yourself about things at home and at work. They also let family and colleagues know what is happening or what needs to be done. The other good thing about notice boards is that they can be as bright and colorful as you want. Being organized doesn't mean being dull!

- Before we move on, don't forget one other very important place for putting papers: the wastebasket/trashcan/recycling bin!

Sometimes information is not worth keeping. Each time you receive a piece of paper, ask yourself, "Do I need to keep this?" If you don't, throw it away!

Summary

Now that we've provided some ideas and tips, jot down any that you think you might use. Is there anything you can do right now to improve the way you organize things?

8

Sold Time, Maintenance Time, and Discretionary Time

The objective of this chapter is
to introduce you to the concept
of Sold Time, Maintenance
Time, and Discretionary Time. *

Sold Time is the time that you sell to an employer or, if you are a student, the time you spend studying. It involves exchanging your time for money or for qualifications, which can be regarded as future money. Sold Time extends beyond the actual hours spent at work or college. It includes the time spent in preparation for these: preparation time, homework, travel time, etc.

Maintenance Time is the time spent keeping your life in workable order. It is when you do the tasks that are necessary to maintain yourself: eating, sleeping, etc. It also includes time spent maintaining others: cooking and cleaning, grocery shopping, caring for family members, etc.

Discretionary Time is the time that remains. This is when we can choose how we want to spend our time.

Time Charts

On the pages that follow, you will see three time charts: a Sold Time Chart, a Maintenance Time Chart, and a Discretionary Time Chart. Fill each one in for last week, using your Life Investment Record if necessary.

You will find that some activities are difficult to categorize. For example, cooking, bathing the children, or shop-

---

* This classification of time was developed by Jack Loughary of the University of Oregon.

ping all could be maintenance time or discretionary time; it depends on whether or not you enjoy the activity. Similarly, traveling to a job could be seen as sold time or discretionary time. You will need to decide how to categorize this sort of activity; you may even want to split the time between two sections.

Under each type of time, write down all the activities that fall into that category. Write down the amount of time you spend on each activity for each day of the week.

Add up the daily total for each type of time in the "Total" line at the bottom of each chart.

Then, add up the grand total for each type of time.

Sold Time Chart						
Mon	Tue	Wed	Thu	Fri	Sat	Sun
Total						
				Grand Total		

Maintenance Time Chart						
Mon	Tue	Wed	Thu	Fri	Sat	Sun
Total						
				Grand Total		

Discretionary Time Chart						
Mon	Tue	Wed	Thu	Fri	Sat	Sun
Total						
				Grand Total		

You now should have a clear picture of

- Your weekly total for each activity.
- Your daily totals for the three different types of time.
- Your week's grand total for each type of time.

Here is what Michael's completed charts looked like.

Michael's Sold Time Chart

Mon	Tue	Wed	Thu	Fri	Sat	Sun
7:40, travel to work 8:30-5:30 work Travel home, 40 minutes Work at home, one hour	7:30-8:30, work (incl. travel time)	7:30-5:45 + travel (40 mins.) Work at home, 1 hour	7:30-5:20, working Travel home, 40 mins.	7:30-5:40, incl. travel home		
Total 11 hrs., 50 m.	13 hrs.	11 hrs., 50 m.	10 hrs., 30 m.	10 hrs., 10 m.	None	None
				Grand Total		57 hrs. 20 m.

Michael's Maintenance Time Chart

Mon	Tue	Wed	Thu	Fri	Sat	Sun
7, got up Get ready, 20 mins. Breakfast, 15 mins. Bed, 10 p.m.	6:30, got up Get ready, 1 hr. No evening meal (big lunch) Bed, 9 p.m.	7, got up Get ready, 35 mins. Shopping in evening, 1 hr. Bed, 9 p.m.	6:30-7:30, get ready, go to work Get ready to go out, 6:50-7:30 p.m. Bed, 12 a.m.	7, got up Evening meal, 1 hr. Bed, 10:30 p.m.	9 a.m., got up, bath, 10:30 a.m. Lunch, 1.5 hrs. Dinner, 1 hr. Bed 10:30 p.m.	10:30, got up Brunch, 1 hr. Clean car, 1 hr. Cook & eat meal, 1.75 hrs. Bed, 11 p.m.
Total 10 hrs. 5 m.	9 hrs., 30 m.	11 hrs., 35 m.	11 hrs.	8 hrs.	14.5 hrs.	16.75 hrs.
				Grand Total		81 hrs., 25 m.

If you could compare your totals for sold time, maintenance time, and discretionary time with those of other people, you would find significant variations. If possible, persuade some of your friends or colleagues to complete time charts so that you can compare them with yours. People live their lives very differently. There is no right or wrong pattern. A mother of five will have a very different pattern from a retired single man. However, within individual patterns there usually is some room for adjustment. Where this is possible, most of us would choose to increase discretionary time because that is the time where we can choose what we really want to do. It is our leisure time.

Michael's Discretionary Time Chart						
Mon	Tue	Wed	Thu	Fri	Sat	Sun
Out for evening meal, 2 hrs.	T.V., 1/2 hr.	Talked and drank at home, 1.5 hrs.	Went out for meal, 4.5 hrs.	Records, 1.5 hrs. T.V., coffee, 1 hr., 20 min. Guitar 2 hrs. Write letters, 1 hr., 20 mins.	Holiday prep., 1.5 hr. Buy gifts, 3 hrs. Assemble VCR, 1.5 hrs. DIY kit, 4 hrs.	Holiday decor. & food, 3 hrs. Make fire, 1/2 hr. Parents visit, 1.5 hrs. Read, 1.5 hrs.
Total 2 hrs.	1/2 hr.	1.5 hrs.	4.5 hrs.	6 hrs., 10 m.	9 hrs.	6.5 hrs.
				Grand Total		30 hrs., 10 m.

Look over your three time charts. Are there any changes you can make in sold and maintenance time to increase your discretionary time? Write any ideas in the following space.

Changes I Could Make to Increase My Discretionary Time

Summary

An increase in discretionary time requires a reduction in maintenance time and sold time. We could choose to neglect our personal appearance to have more time for conversation and reading, but for most of us this would not be acceptable. One way of increasing discretionary time is by performing our sold time and maintenance time activities more efficiently, that is, in less time.

The next chapter will help you to identify Time Cheaters and Time Beaters. With an understanding of these, you should have more time to do the things you want.

9

Time Cheaters
and How to
Stop Them

The objective of this chapter is
to help you to identify your
Time Cheaters and to find ways
to beat them.

Time Cheaters come in all shapes and sizes; they can be physical and mental; they can be created by you or imposed on you by other people. The important thing is to become aware of them; then you can learn to deal with them.

Spend some time thinking about the things that stop or hinder you from doing the things that you want or need to do. Is there a neighbor or colleague who keeps you talking? Do you try to do too many things at the same time? Is your office or workroom disorganized? Write down any Time Cheaters that come to mind.

Time Cheaters

Time Cheaters and Time Beaters

You may find it difficult to identify your own particular Time Cheaters, or perhaps there are too many to mention! Look at the following list of Time Cheaters and, for each one, ask, "Is this me?" If it is one of your Time Cheaters, place a check mark in the box and look at the possible solutions, or Time Beaters, that we've given.

Time Cheater	Is This Me?	Time Beater
I spend too much time talking to people who won't go away.	☐	Learn to be firm; say "I don't mean to be rude but I must get back to my work."
I get sidetracked easily and lack self-discipline.	☐	Make action plans and stick to them. Promise yourself a reward for good timekeeping.
My colleagues/friends/kids interrupt me all the time.	☐	Tell everyone that you don't want to be disturbed. Have regular "quiet" periods that people know about and respect.
I take on too much work.	☐	Learn to say "No" politely but firmly. You may benefit from some assertiveness training.
Time runs out! I'm always rushed and late.	☐	Really think about what you have to do and how long it will take. Then add 20 percent extra time to form a "time cushion."
I get panicky and try to do everything at once.	☐	Prioritize! Spend five minutes quietly figuring out what jobs must be done and what can wait. Start at the top of your list and work through it steadily.
I spend hours looking for papers and files.	☐	You need to get organized. Read through Chapter 7 and start trying different filing and sorting systems.

Summary

Can you think of any changes that you can make or actions you can take to prevent Time Cheaters? Write them down in the box that follows.

In the next chapter, we offer more ways of saving time.

10

Saving Time

The objective of this chapter is
to discover ways to save time.

A s pointed out in Chapter 8, we can increase discretionary time by saving time spent on other activities. This leaves us more time to do the things we want to do. Alternatively, we can increase our workload without increasing sold time by performing work tasks more efficiently. Aside from knowing what we want to do now and doing it, there is no simple rule for saving time. Effective time use comes from examining our activities and finding ways of eliminating them or doing them more quickly.

Take the next five minutes to write down all the ideas you can think of for saving time. At this stage, don't structure the ideas or evaluate them. If you can get someone else to share ideas with you, so much the better.

Personal Project

Now go back over your ideas and decide which ones you think are most useful. Write these into your personal planner and work them into your planning activities.

Some Useful Time Beaters

The following are some Time Beaters that we have found useful. Add your own at the end.

- Use waiting time! If you ever find yourself waiting for a bus, an appointment, etc., don't think of it as a *waste* of time but as a *gift* of time. Use it constructively: to relax, to ponder a decision, to review your daily checklist, to read a book, to do a crossword puzzle, or numerous other things! Always carry a pen and paper and a book to read.

- Make your daily checklists and prioritize your activities. You are then less likely to spend time on C-list activities.

- Establish deadlines, write them in your personal planner, and keep them.

- Combine activities; for example, discuss a business-related matter with your colleague over lunch.

- Have a place for everything and keep everything in its place. If something is worth having, it's worth knowing where it is when you want it!

- Make yourself a filing system. You need something to hold the files (folders) and something to hold the folders (a large box or filing cabinet).

- Remember your first filing option is the trash. Do you really need that piece of paper? What is the worst thing that could happen if you didn't have it?

- Handle each piece of paper only once; deal with it the first time you pick it up.
- Always keep a notebook with you. Don't lose an idea because you had nowhere to record it. Think on paper.
- Reinforce your time-saving efforts. Reward yourself with something you really want when you have completed a task.
- If flexitime is available to you, use it to travel to work at off-peak times; save traveling time.
- Delegate as much as you can.
- Value your discretionary time the same as your paid time. Is the time you spend traveling to a less expensive store always worth the money saved?
- If you can afford a dishwasher, washing machine, microwave oven, or freezer, get one!
- Constantly ask yourself, "Is this the best use of my time right now?"

Now review your list. Put an X next to all the ideas you find useful and list them in your planner.

Summary

You might be starting to feel as if all the spontaneity has been planned out of your life! But you will have more time to take things as they come if you plan the things you have to do. Time management aims to make you more relaxed and gives you more time to relax in.

11

Leisure Time

*The objective of this chapter is
to help you to identify your leisure needs and determine the
activities that best meet them.*

Earlier, we suggested that our time can be separated into sold time, maintenance time, and discretionary time, and that discretionary time is the time available for us to choose what we do, the time available for leisure. In this chapter, we look at this open-ended resource, how to choose to fill it, and how to identify the many needs it can fill.

First, let's look at the amount of time available to us as discretionary time. Is there any way of increasing it by cutting down on sold time and maintenance time? One way of dramatically altering the balance between sold time and discretionary time is to convert discretionary activities into sold activities, much as musicians or professional athletes do.

Even if you can't make a career of your hobby, there will be ways to increase your discretionary time by a more ordered, efficient approach to your sold activities and maintenance activities. Look back at Chapter 10 and then in the space that follows write down three ways that you can increase your available discretionary time.

1. _____

2. _____

3. _____

After you have reduced your sold time and maintenance time as much as is practical, you will have expanded your discretionary time to its maximum in your present circumstances.

The only way you can now increase your leisure satisfaction is by making choices. Your Leisure Pie is as big as it can be; you have now to decide what ingredients will make it the best for you. First, it would be useful to get a clear idea of what leisure means to you.

In the space that follows, write as many definitions of leisure as you can think of in five minutes. Don't try to organize your ideas, let them flow freely. If you can get someone to do this with you, so much the better.

Here are some definitions that occurred to us:

- Leisure is attractive only when we choose it.
- Leisure time includes play time, enjoyed for its own sake.
- Leisure time is time at your disposal after paid work and activities such as eating and sleeping (maintenance activities) have been done.
- Leisure time is recreation time—time out from paid work to recharge your emotional, physical, and intellectual batteries.
- Leisure and unemployment: We cannot ignore the concept of "enforced leisure" and its attendant difficulties.
- Leisure time is positive time. You can exercise powerful choice in its use. You can enjoy it at whatever level you choose.

• Your choice of leisure activity is entirely individual; reasons for doing it are subjective and complex. For instance, playing tennis is a physical activity that is enjoyed for its sense of coordinated motion until you get so good at it that you are paid to do it. Then it is a job. Amateur tennis can lead to meeting people, which makes it a social pastime—although some people use it as an opportunity to make business contacts.

An important point is that leisure time is pleasure time. It's not leisure if you didn't choose it. Enjoyment and choice are central to leisure.

What Do You Enjoy Most?

If you have a clear idea about what types of leisure activities you enjoy, you will be in a better position to make choices among different activities. The following questionnaire is designed to help you to identify the features of the leisure activities you enjoy most.

Leisure Quotient Questionnaire

Directions: Read each statement carefully and decide whether you agree or disagree with it. Use the following scale to rank your answer.

1	2	3	4	5
Strongly disagree	Disagree	Not sure	Agree	Strongly agree

Interest Group A: Being With People

1	2	3	4	5	I enjoy being in a crowd
1	2	3	4	5	I like talking to people
1	2	3	4	5	Who I'm with is more important than what I'm doing
1	2	3	4	5	I like joining clubs

Add up your score   Total =

Interest Group B: Being With Family

1	2	3	4	5	I like to plan family outings
1	2	3	4	5	I enjoy evenings when the family gets together to talk and relax
1	2	3	4	5	I get on well with all generations in my family
1	2	3	4	5	I miss members of my family when we have to spend a long time apart

Add up your score   Total =

Interest Group C: Being Alone

1	2	3	4	5	I enjoy my own company
1	2	3	4	5	I like being able to concentrate on something without stopping to talk
1	2	3	4	5	I enjoy having a room or space of my own
1	2	3	4	5	I like to rely on my own judgment

Add up your score   Total =

Interest Group D: Using Your Brain

1	2	3	4	5	I enjoy time to think, plan, and decide
1	2	3	4	5	I jump at an idea and like to follow it up for myself
1	2	3	4	5	I like reading and learning new facts
1	2	3	4	5	I enjoy discussing problems and issues

Add up your score   Total =

Interest Group E: Making Something

1	2	3	4	5	I like to see an end product for my efforts
1	2	3	4	5	I enjoy using my hands
1	2	3	4	5	I feel happy working with tools and machines
1	2	3	4	5	I like physical activity

Add up your score   Total =

Interest Group F: Helping Others

1	2	3	4	5	I like to feel useful
1	2	3	4	5	I like showing other people how to solve problems
1	2	3	4	5	I enjoy giving some of my time to good causes
1	2	3	4	5	I think we're here to help other people feel better

Add up your score   Total =

Interest Group G: Being Different

1	2	3	4	5	I like to stand out in a crowd
1	2	3	4	5	I enjoy doing the opposite from what people expect
1	2	3	4	5	I like to make up my own mind
1	2	3	4	5	I like exploring new ways of doing things

Add up your score   Total =

Interest Group H: Exercising

1	2	3	4	5	I like to be very fit
1	2	3	4	5	I enjoy physical activity
1	2	3	4	5	I like being outdoors
1	2	3	4	5	I like to meet difficult physical challenges

Add up your score   Total =

Interest Group I: Being Creative

1	2	3	4	5	I like to use my imagination
1	2	3	4	5	I like to express myself through art, crafts, music, or writing (score for any of these)
1	2	3	4	5	I like to daydream
1	2	3	4	5	I like being in an environment where people are using their imaginations

Add up your score   Total =

Interest Group J: Competing With Others

1 2 3 4 5   I enjoy winning

1 2 3 4 5   I like to do things to the best of my ability

1 2 3 4 5   I like to find out if I can do things better than other people

1 2 3 4 5   Being second isn't good enough

Add up your score   Total =

Interest Group K: Appreciating Nature

1 2 3 4 5   I prefer the country to the city

1 2 3 4 5   I enjoy seeing beautiful scenery

1 2 3 4 5   I like to learn about nature from books and television programs

1 2 3 4 5   I like animals and plants

Add up your score   Total =

Interest Group L: Escaping From Stress

1 2 3 4 5   I like to find ways to "wind down" after work

1 2 3 4 5   I like things that take my attention away from problems

1 2 3 4 5   I like to take off on the spur of the moment and do something unexpected

1 2 3 4 5   Relaxing is as important as working

Add up your score   Total =

Interest Group M: Being Entertained

1 2 3 4 5   I like being a member of an audience

1 2 3 4 5   I like looking out for events that I can go to

1 2 3 4 5   I like sitting back and being taken out of myself by a sports event, concert, film, play, or television program

1 2 3 4 5   I like talking about an event I've enjoyed

Add up your score   Total =

Add up your score for each interest group. Now rank your groups in order, putting the interest group with the highest score first, and so on.

Order	Group Letter	Score
1.		
2.		
3.		
4.		
5.		
6.		
7.		
8.		
9.		
10.		
11.		
12.		
13.		

Draw a line under the first three groups. These are your main leisure types.

If you score high in groups **A B C F G I J K L M**, look at leisure activities to meet your emotional and social needs—how you feel and how you relate to others.

If you score high in groups **E H K L**, look at activities that are geared to your physical needs—how your body feels.

If you score high in groups **C D E I M**, look at activities that satisfy your intellectual needs—activities that stimulate your mind.

Are you surprised by your leisure needs as shown by your Leisure Quotient Questionnaire?

People in each of the three leisure types have leisure activities that suit them best. The following is a list of activities corresponding to each group. Take your three highest-scoring groups and look at the activities suggested for each of these groups on the Leisure Time Table.

Leisure Activities Table

Group A: Being With People		
Amusement parks	Dancing	Restaurants
Antique shows	Football	Shopping
Art class	Golf	Tennis
Bowling	Movies	Theater
Camping	Museums	Zoos
Cards	Night school	
Clubs	Parks	

Group B: Being With Family		
Bicycling	Hiking	Reading
Board games	Holidays	Stamp collecting
Boating	Jigsaw puzzles	Table tennis
Camping	Model making	Television
Cooking	Museums	Zoos
Fishing	Neighborhood restaurant	

Group C: Being Alone		
Bird watching	Painting	Swimming
Coin/stamp collecting	Photography	Television
Crossword puzzles	Reading	Woodworking
Jogging	Sewing	Writing
Meditation	Sightseeing	Yoga
Music	Stereo	

Group D: Using Your Brain		
Archaeology	Flying	Night school
Art galleries	Genealogy	Reading
Astronomy	Inventing	Sailing
Book clubs	Lectures	Travel
Chess	Museums	Word puzzles

Group E: Making Something

Baking	Nature collections	Sewing
Designing	Painting	Weaving
Gardening	Pottery	Wine making
Knitting	Restoring antiques	Woodworking
Leather craft	Scrapbooks	Writing
Model making	Sculpture	

Group F: Helping Others

Babysitting	Environmentalism	Repairs
Charity sales	Giving a massage	Sponsored events
Driving	Listening	Volunteer work
Entertaining	"Meals on Wheels"	

Group G: Being Different

Hang gliding	Rock climbing
Performance art	Skydiving

Group H: Exercising

Athletics/sports	Ice skating	Tennis
Bicycling	Jogging	Volleyball
Calisthenics/aerobics	Racquet sports	Weightlifting
Canoeing	Skiing	Yoga
Dancing	Soccer	
Horseback riding	Swimming	

Group I: Being Creative

Acting	Flower arranging	Pottery
Carving	Gardening	Sculpture
Choreography	Leather craft	Sketching
Composing	Model making	Weaving
Cooking/baking	Needlework	Writing
Decorating	Painting	
Directing	Photography	

Group J: Competing With Others		
Animal showing	Boxing	Golf
Archery	Cards	Racing
Baseball	Chess	Soccer
Basketball	Dance contests	Tennis
Board games	Exhibiting	Weight lifting
Bowling	Football	

Group K: Appreciating Nature		
Archaeology	Geology	Rock climbing
Astronomy	Hiking	Sailing
Beachcombing	Landscaping	Sketching
Camping	Nature programs	Walking
Fishing	Parks	Zoos
Gardening	Riding	

Group L: Escaping From Stress		
Amusement parks	Parks	Television
Having a massage	Physical activity	Travel
Jogging	Radio	Visiting
Movies	Reading	Walking
Painting	Sunbathing	

Group M: Being Entertained		
Ballet	Movies	Stereo
Circus	Reading	Television
Concerts	Sightseeing	Theater
Conversation	Spectator sports	

Leisure Activity Advantages and Disadvantages

Explore each of the activities listed in your three highest-scoring groups. Use the chart below to evaluate them by weighing the advantages and disadvantages of each one. This offers you the opportunity to consider new leisure activities suited to your leisure type that you might not have thought about before.

Leisure Activity	Advantages	Disadvantages

Here is an example of one person's chart:

Leisure Activity	Advantages	Disadvantages
Archery	New skill Outdoor activity Meet new people Romantic Can rent equipment Exercise	Cost of equipment Traveling time Dangerous Never done it before
Card games	Win money Meet people Play anywhere	I always lose I gamble recklessly Boring Gets in the way of talking Don't like sitting still!

Look over your chart and circle the new activities for which the advantages outweigh the disadvantages. Include these new leisure activities into planning your discretionary time. Look carefully at your stated disadvantages. Reactions such as "boring" and "take too much time" often conceal the real reasons we don't like to admit to ourselves. Saying that something is boring often means that we don't have the skills to do it successfully. If we acknowledge that we don't have the skills, we are in a position to begin to acquire them.

In the space below, write a list of ten things you enjoy doing.

1. _____
2. _____
3. _____
4. _____
5. _____
6. _____
7. _____
8. _____
9. _____
10. _____

How I can start doing more_____now?

_____

_____

How I can start doing more_____now?

_____

_____

How I can start doing more_____now?

_____

_____

Another way to expand your leisure choices is to look for events in your local newspaper. Buy a paper, read through it, and underline activities you have not done before and would like to do. You also can try libraries and community centers, as they usually have schedules of many different activities going on in your area. Set yourself a target to do one new thing each week for the next four weeks. Write these new activities into your monthly plan.

Four things I will do or see in the next month

1. _____
2. _____
3. _____
4. _____

Summary

In this chapter, you have identified your own leisure needs and explored new choices for your leisure. You have acquired the skills and techniques for evaluating these new leisure activities throughout this program. Given that your discretionary time is limited, you will have to choose between your leisure activities, both new and old. As always, prioritizing activities is our guide to making the best of leisure time.

In the space below, list your leisure choices for next week and prioritize them.

_____

_____

_____

When you've done this, fit in your leisure priorities alongside the other activities in your diary.

12

Program
Review

The objective of this chapter is
to review your gains from time
management.

Time management means organizing yourself better to get what *you* want from your time. Its aim is not to fill up your life with activity! It is to help you to identify what you want out of life and to plan how to go about getting it, so you know what to do to achieve what you want in life. You have been introduced to, and have used, a number of techniques to achieve this. This is a good time to reevaluate these techniques. Read through the list of techniques that you have used in the program. Think about whether or not the techniques have worked for you and write down why you found them successful or why you think they didn't suit you.

Time Investment Techniques

Life Investment Record (page 9)

_____

_____

Time Diary and Rank Order Activity Charts (pages 11-12)

_____

_____

Satisfaction and Actual-Time Pie Comparisons (pages 23-25)

_____

_____

Priorities for This Week (page 31)

_____

_____

List Making (page 35)

_____

_____

List Prioritizing (page 36)

_____

_____

Using a Diary (page 42)

_____

_____

Using a Planner (page 43)

_____

_____

Creating an Efficient Working Environment (page 48)

_____

_____

Time Cheaters (page 62)

_____

_____

Time Beaters (page 63)

_____

_____

Final Comment: Time Management Now

We hope that you have enjoyed working through this book and that you have achieved what you wanted from it.

Look back at your personal objectives. Has your thinking changed since then? If it has, write down your new ideas about time in the following space.

_____

_____

_____

Now is a good time to review what you have gained and start applying it!

In the space below, list three things that you have learned from this workbook about yourself and the way that you manage your time.

1. _____

2. _____

3. _____

Now list three techniques to improve the way you manage your time that you have learned as a result of doing this workbook.

1. _____

2. _____

3. _____

Remember, the goal is not to make a plan and stick to it but to create a plan and constantly ask the question: Is this working? If it is not, it's time to revise the plan.

Try to reserve some time every month to review how you are using your time. Write it in your planner to make sure you make time!

You have now reached the end of this time-management workbook. You may find that you need to refresh your memory from time to time; just go over some of the sections you found most useful. We hope that you have enjoyed this book and that you will have fun putting your new skills into action.

"To Choose Time Is to Save Time."

— Francis Bacon

Appendix

Weekly Calendar:

	Monday	Tuesday	Wednesday	Thursday	Friday	Saturday	Sunday
Morning							
Afternoon							
Evening							

Monday, October 15

6AM	
7AM	
8AM	
9AM	
10AM	
11AM	
NOON	
1PM	
2PM	
3PM	
4PM	
5PM	
6PM	
7PM	
8PM	
9PM	
10PM	
11PM	
MIDNIGHT	

Action
Talk To
Telephone
Write To

Notes

About the Authors

Dr. Barrie Hopson

Barrie is joint chairman of Lifeskills Learning Ltd. Previously he founded the Counseling and Career Development Unit at Leeds University and was the first director until 1984. He has worked widely as a consultant to industrial and educational organizations in the United Kingdom, the United States of America, and Europe. He was responsible for setting up the first career counseling service in British industry in 1970 (at Imperial Chemical Industry) and has since helped a number of organizations in different countries to set up career counseling and career management systems. He is a professional associate of the National Training Laboratories for Applied Behavioral Science in Washington, D.C., a fellow of the British Psychological Society, and of the British Institute of Management.

He has written twenty-two books and numerous articles on personal and career development, marriage, lifeskills teaching, quality service, transition, and change management and generic training skills.

Mike Scally

Mike is joint chairman of Lifeskills Learning Ltd. He combines management training with writing and lecturing. He was Deputy Director of the Counseling and Career Development Unit at Leeds University in 1976 and was involved with its training programs and national projects until 1984.

He has extensive training experience with many of the United Kingdom's major companies and an international reputation in the field of education. He serves on the management committees of and is consultant to many national groups—promoting development education and training at home and abroad.

Mike Scally has written twelve books and many articles on career management, customer service, and lifeskills teaching.